Joe Grows Tomatoes

Anders Hanson

Consulting Editor, Diane Craig, M.A./Reading Specialist

Published by ABDO Publishing Company, 4940 Viking Drive, Edina, Minnesota 55435.

Printed in the United States.

Credits
Edited by: Pam Price
Curriculum Coordinator: Nancy Tuminelly
Cover and Interior Design and Production: Mighty Media
Photo and Illustration Credits: Brand X Pictures, Corbis Images, Digital Vision, Anders Hanson, Hemera, Tracy Kompelien, PhotoDisc, Rubberball Productions

Library of Congress Cataloging-in-Publication Data

Hanson, Anders, 1980-
    Joe grows tomatoes / Anders Hanson.
      p. cm. -- (Rhyme time)
    Includes index.
    ISBN 1-59197-796-7 (hardcover)
    ISBN 1-59197-902-1 (paperback)
    1. English language--Rhyme--Juvenile literature. I. Title. II. Rhyme time (ABDO Publishing Company)

PE1517.H37545 2005
808.1--dc22
                                                                                2004049040

SandCastle™ books are created by a professional team of educators, reading specialists, and content developers around five essential components that include phonemic awareness, phonics, vocabulary, text comprehension, and fluency. All books are written, reviewed, and leveled for guided reading, early intervention reading, and Accelerated Reader® programs and designed for use in shared, guided, and independent reading and writing activities to support a balanced approach to literacy instruction.

Let Us Know

After reading the book, SandCastle would like you to tell us your stories about reading. What is your favorite page? Was there something hard that you needed help with? Share the ups and downs of learning to read. We want to hear from you! To get posted on the ABDO Publishing Company Web site, send us e-mail at:

sandcastle@abdopub.com

SandCastle Level: Fluent

Words that rhyme do not have to be spelled the same. These words rhyme with each other:

buffaloes

knows

compose

rows

foes

scarecrows

grows

sows

hoes

tomatoes

Madison and Brian run through a field where long grass **grows**.

The **buffaloes** are crossing the stream.

José will do well on the test because he **knows** the answers.

Alexis is a good violin player.

She is playing a song that she helped compose.

Dan plays checkers with Emma.

The checkerboard has **rows** of red and black squares.

Christian is dressed up as a superhero.

He pretends to fight **foes**.

Farmers put **scarecrows** in their fields to keep birds from eating the crops.

The hardware store sells gardening tools, such as rakes and **hoes**.

Samantha hopes to grow healthy vegetables from the seeds she **sows**.

Sarah helps her mom pick tomatoes.

Joe Grows Tomatoes

Joe grows tomatoes.

Joe plants the seeds in even rows.

He waters every seed he sows.

He makes scarecrows
to frighten the tomatoes' foes.

But still those tomatoes rose
no higher than Joe's toes.

Joe's friend Rose
said, "Everybody knows
that tomatoes grow better
to music you compose."

They wrote a song with highs and lows and played it on their new oboes.

After hearing the oboes,
each tiny tomato grows,
until they're as big as buffaloes!

Now Joe goes to gardening shows to pose with those tomatoes.

He is so happy that he glows!

Rhyming Riddle

What do you call a bison's gardening tools?

Buffalo's hoes

22

Glossary

buffalo. an oxlike animal such as the water buffalo or the African buffalo; the North American bison is commonly called a buffalo

compose. to create an artistic work, such as a poem or a song

foe. enemy

hoe. a garden tool with a long handle and a thin blade that is used for weeding or loosening soil

oboe. a woodwind instrument with a double reed

sow. to scatter seeds over the ground so they will grow

About SandCastle™

A professional team of educators, reading specialists, and content developers created the SandCastle™ series to support young readers as they develop reading skills and strategies and increase their general knowledge. The SandCastle™ series has four levels that correspond to early literacy development in young children. The levels are provided to help teachers and parents select the appropriate books for young readers.

Emerging Readers
(no flags)

Beginning Readers
(1 flag)

Transitional Readers
(2 flags)

Fluent Readers
(3 flags)

These levels are meant only as a guide. All levels are subject to change.

To see a complete list of SandCastle™ books and other nonfiction titles from ABDO Publishing Company, visit **www.abdopub.com** or contact us at:
4940 Viking Drive, Edina, Minnesota 55435 • 1-800-800-1312 • fax: 1-952-831-1632